# Little Jackrabbit

## AT HOME IN THE DESERT

WRITTEN BY JIM STRICKLER
ILLUSTRATED BY KAREN PRITCHETT

Publications International, Ltd.

**O**n a warm morning in the spring, Mother Jackrabbit is working quietly under the thick sagebrush. She is using her paw to scrape out a smooth spot in the dry, sandy soil.

Mother Jackrabbit covers the spot with some of her own fur to make a soft bed. Tucked under the sagebrush, the little bed is hidden from other animals.

When the soft bed is ready, Mother Jackrabbit gives birth to three tiny babies. There are two girls and one boy. The boy jackrabbit is named Baby Jack.

Like his mother, Baby Jack has bright eyes, smooth brown fur, and a nose that constantly twitches. His big ears bounce up and down as he hops around the desert.

Even though he is young, Baby Jack is eager to explore his new world. His large ears pick up many wonderful sounds: the songs of a meadowlark, the barking of a prairie dog, and the "hooooo" of the wind blowing across the dry land.

As he sniffs the air, he enjoys smelling the sagebrush and the sweet cactus flowers.

During the hot desert days, Baby Jack does not explore. Like his mother, he sits still in the cool shade of a clump of grass.

He feels safe in the shade. His brown fur blends right in with the soil and the dry grass. Hungry coyotes and eagles that are hunting for food cannot see him easily.

In the desert, almost every day is bright, dry, and sunny. But this afternoon, Baby Jack watches gray clouds gather in the sky. The day gets cooler and darker. Then, Baby Jack feels drops of water coming from above. It is raining!

Rainy days are rare in the dry desert. The rain is new to Baby Jack.

The rainfall changes the way the desert looks. It makes all the plants blossom. Instead of being brown and dry, the desert is now filled with many different kinds of colorful flowers.

Baby Jack explores the desert and sees things that he has never seen before. He is amazed to see so many beautiful colors: yellow, orange, pink, and purple.

As the bright sun begins to set each evening, Baby Jack and his family search for food. He hops from plant to plant, nibbling on grasses. With his sharp teeth, he can eat almost anything.

Mother Jackrabbit teaches Baby Jack to chew a hole in a cactus. He avoids the prickly spines on the outside and eats the moist part inside.

After Baby Jack enjoys his tasty cactus meal, he and his mother do some more exploring. Mother Jackrabbit's powerful sense of smell helps her sniff out danger. She can smell a coyote approaching.

Baby Jack is playing around in the dirt when his mother sees the coyote watching them from a nearby rock.

Baby Jack hears a loud "Thumpa, thumpa, thumpa!" Mother Jackrabbit is pounding one of her back paws against the hard ground.

Mother Jackrabbit is trying to tell Baby Jack and the other jackrabbits that danger is near. Baby Jack knows that it means he should hide. He immediately darts under a bushy plant.

The coyote leaves when he can't find the hiding jackrabbits. Baby Jack tenses his powerful leg muscles. Then—whoosh— he is off! He bounds away to meet up with his family.